LET'S EXPLORE THE STATES

Rocky Mountain

Colorado
Utah
Wyoming

Dan Harvey

Mason Crest
450 Parkway Drive, Suite D
Broomall, PA 19008
www.masoncrest.com

©2016 by Mason Crest, an imprint of National Highlights, Inc.

Printed and bound in the United States of America.

CPSIA Compliance Information: Batch #LES2015.
For further information, contact Mason Crest at 1-866-MCP-Book.

First printing
1 3 5 7 9 8 6 4 2

Library of Congress Cataloging-in-Publication Data

Harvey, Dan, 1954-
  Rocky Mountain : Colorado, Utah, Wyoming / Dan Harvey.
      pages cm. — (Let's explore the states)
  Includes bibliographical references and index.
  ISBN 978-1-4222-3332-0 (hc)
  ISBN 978-1-4222-8617-3 (ebook)
  1. West (U.S.)—Juvenile literature. 2. Colorado—Juvenile literature.
  3. Utah—Juvenile literature. 4. Wyoming (U.S.)—Juvenile literature. I. Title.
  F591.H275 2015
  978—dc23
                                    2014050187

Let's Explore the States series ISBN: 978-1-4222-3319-1

Publisher's Note: Websites listed in this book were active at the time of publication. The publisher is not responsible for websites that have changed their address or discontinued operation since the date of publication. The publisher reviews and updates the websites each time the book is reprinted.

About the Author: Dan Harvey is a freelance writer based in Wilmington, Delaware. He has won six national journalism awards and is the author of several books. He is a frequent contributor to national magazines focused on medical technology, industrial technology, business, current events and history.

Table of Contents

KEY ICONS TO LOOK FOR:

Words to Understand: These words with their easy-to-understand definitions will increase the reader's understanding of the text, while building vocabulary skills.

Sidebars: This boxed material within the main text allows readers to build knowledge, gain insights, explore possibilities, and broaden their perspectives by weaving together additional information to provide realistic and holistic perspectives.

Research Projects: Readers are pointed toward areas of further inquiry connected to each chapter. Suggestions are provided for projects that encourage deeper research and analysis.

Text-Dependent Questions: These questions send the reader back to the text for more careful attention to the evidence presented there.

Series Glossary of Key Terms: This back-of-the book glossary contains terminology used throughout this series. Words found here increase the reader's ability to read and comprehend higher-level books and articles in this field.

LET'S EXPLORE THE STATES

Atlantic: North Carolina, Virginia, West Virginia
Central Mississippi River Basin: Arkansas, Iowa, Missouri
East South-Central States: Kentucky, Tennessee
Eastern Great Lakes: Indiana, Michigan, Ohio
Gulf States: Alabama, Louisiana, Mississippi
Lower Atlantic: Florida, Georgia, South Carolina
Lower Plains: Kansas, Nebraska
Mid-Atlantic: Delaware, District of Columbia, Maryland
Non-Continental: Alaska, Hawaii
Northern New England: Maine, New Hampshire, Vermont
Northeast: New Jersey, New York, Pennsylvania
Northwest: Idaho, Oregon, Washington
Rocky Mountain: Colorado, Utah, Wyoming
Southern New England: Connecticut, Massachusetts, Rhode Island
Southwest: New Mexico, Oklahoma, Texas
U.S. Territories and Possessions
Upper Plains: Montana, North Dakota, South Dakota
The West: Arizona, California, Nevada
Western Great Lakes: Illinois, Minnesota, Wisconsin

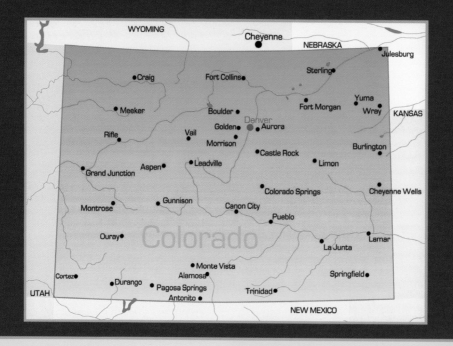

Colorado at a Glance

Area: 104,094 sq miles (269,602 sq km). 8th largest state[1]
  Land: 103,641 sq mi (268,429 sq km)
  Water: 454 sq mi (1,176 sq km)
Highest elevation: Mount Elbert, 14,433 feet (4,399 m)
Lowest elevation: Arkansas River, 3,315 feet (1,010 m)

Statehood: August 1, 1876 (38th state)
Capital: Denver

Pop.: 5,355,866 (22nd largest state)[2]

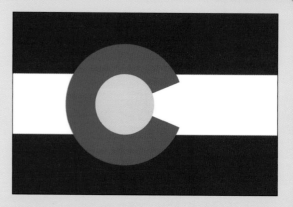

State nickname: the Centennial State
State bird: lark bunting
State flower: alpine columbine

[1] *U.S. Census Bureau*
[2] *U.S. Census Bureau, 2014 estimate*

Colorado

The natural beauty of Colorado seems to inspire artistic expression. In 1972, singer John Denver released a song about the state called "Rocky Mountain High." The hit record served as a celebration of Colorado's natural wonders, and became one of the state's official songs in 2007. The inspiration for this song is understandable to anyone who has ever lived in or visited Colorado.

The word *Colorado* means "colored red." During the 18th century, Spanish explorers observed that a river coursing from the mountains had a reddish tint due to silt. That river became known as the Colorado River, and the surrounding area became known as Colorado.

Geography

By area, Colorado is the eighth-largest of the 50 U.S. states, covering 104,094 square miles (269,602 square kilometers). While Colorado is best known for its mountains, the state has many diverse geographic features and regions, including plains, desert,

plateaus, *buttes*, and forests.

When you look at Colorado on a map, you see an almost-perfect rectangular shape. One of its corners is part of the famous "Four Corners," meaning that it meets a common geographic location with Arizona, New Mexico and Utah. This corner is considered the heart of the "American Southwest." This geographic placement provides the state of Colorado with a unique tourist attraction: With the "Four Corners" borders, and with strategic feet placement, it is possible for a visitor to stand in four states at the same time.

Colorado is noted for its high elevation. Its capital city Denver is called the "Mile High City," due to its elevation 5,280 feet (1,609 m) above sea level. To the city's left is a mountainous territory that boasts high-rising

Words to Understand in This Chapter

butte—an isolated high hill with a flat top and very steep sides that is usually found in the southwestern region of the United States.

climate—relating to the prevailing weather conditions (temperature, precipitation, storm patterns) in a specific geographic area.

ecologic—pertaining to ecology, or the relationship between organisms and their environment and how natural forces affect this relationship.

extinct—no longer in existence.

foothills—low hills that are situated at the base of higher geographic terrain such as mountains.

hub—a center of business activity in a region.

plateau—a large, flat area of land that rises higher than the surrounding areas.

pueblo—a communal structure, where many people lived, erected by agriculture-based Native American tribes in the southwest.

Buffalo graze on the grassy high plains of Colorado.

Pine forests and snow-capped mountain peaks can be seen at Boreas Pass.

peaks with heights that give Colorado the highest mean elevation in the United States. Many of the peaks rise more than 10,000 feet (3,050 m) above sea level. One of the highest is Pikes Peak, at 14,115 feet (4,302 m). This peak was named in 1806 for its discoverer, Lieutenant Zebulon M. Pike. But the highest peak in all of the Rocky Mountains range—which extends from Western Canada and down into New Mexico—is Colorado's Mount Elbert, which measures 14,433 feet (4,399 m) high.

However, the state's terrain isn't all about majestic height. Its mountains dwarf a wide, flat expanse: the state's eastern portion which encompasses almost one half of its total area. This portion is part of the High Plains,

Red iron peaks are reflected in a high mountain lake off the San Juan Skyway.

which is a significant portion of the Great Plains. In this lower-elevation territory, farmlands form an agrarian patchwork quilt of fields filled with corn, hay, oats, soybeans and wheat. Some farmers in this region also raise livestock. The state's lowest point is found in this eastern area, where the Arikaree River flows from Yuma County, Colorado and into Cheyenne County, Kansas.

The Central portion of the state is where the Rocky Mountains begin to rise from the landscape, starting with *foothills*. The mountainous territory, which runs from north to south, includes the easterly Front Range and the westerly Park Range. The area also includes the Continental Divide, which extends along the crest of the Rocky Mountains in Colorado's "Western Slope."

Moving to the western portion of the state, on the other side of the mountains, visitors can find the Colorado Plateau. Also in this region is the Grand Valley, which is characterized by its desert terrain.

Because of its natural splendor,

Did You Know?

The players on Major League Baseball teams that face the Colorado Rockies at Coors Field in downtown Denver often complain of shortness of breath due to the city's high elevation.

Colorado is the home of several major national parks. These include the Gunnison National Park, the Mesa Verde National Park, and the Rocky Mountain National Park. The Colorado River originates in Rocky Mountain National Park.

Water flows abundantly throughout Colorado. Because of its size, the state boasts four major rivers including the Colorado River, the Rio Grande, the South Platte, and the Arkansas River.

Due to its diverse geography, Colorado has a complex *climate*. The mountains, plains and deserts can significantly affect local weather conditions. In general, winters in Colorado can be very cold and snowy, especially in the mountainous areas. Summers tend to be rather pleasant, with warm days and cool nights. Average annual rainfall is about 16.6 inches through-out the state.

Record temperature highs and lows vary according to region, so that the average annual temperature ranges from 15° Fahrenheit (–9° Celsius) to 88°F (31°C).

Snowfall is highest in the mountainous areas. Denver, which is the state's most populous city and is close to the Rocky Mountains, records an average annual snowfall of 60 inches (152 cm). This much snow creates problems for Denver's citizens, blocking roadways and closing airports. As late as June, travelers driving on Interstate 25 near Denver can experience heavy hail storms that leave the roadway and surrounding ground covered with white ice that resembles snow.

History

When visitors travel into the northwestern portion of Colorado, they enter a sparsely populated region characterized by rocky hills, canyons and desert. They may experience a sense of pre-history; time seems to stand still. This is appropriate, as the area is home of the state's famous Dinosaur National Monument in the northwest corner, near its border with Utah, where many fossils have been discovered.

The area that eventually became the state of Colorado was home to dinosaurs. Leaving footprint and bone behind were ferocious meat eaters such as the Allosaurus and Torvosuarus, as well as the Stegosaurus and the large sauropods Apatosaurus and Amphicoelias.

Long after the *extinction* of the dinosaurs, humans from Asia known as Paleo-Indians arrived in North America. Anthropologists have determined that the Colorado region was inhabited by Native Americans roughly 13,000 years ago. Many of these early inhabitants were cliff dwellers that built *pueblo*-style homes. Within gaping cliff canyons, inhabitants used local materials, such as rock and adobe mud, to build high-rise homes that protected them from the harsh environment and animal predators.

Meanwhile, an area located on the eastern portion of the Rocky Mountains served as an important migration route. From these early inhabitants arose Native American tribes such as the Utes, Apaches, and Comanche, among others.

During the 16th century, the first Europeans arrived in the Colorado region. In the early 1540s, the Spanish conquistador Francisco Vásquez de Coronado led an expedition through the American southwest. Juan de Ulibarri later claimed the Colorado region for Spain in 1706.

During the 18th century, the rights to Colorado passed from Spain to France in 1740, then back to Spain in 1763, and finally back to France in 1800. During this time there were few Europeans in the region. The only ones were fur trappers and hunters who dealt with the Native Americans that lived in the region.

In 1803, the United States purchased the vast Louisiana territory from France, which included the northern part of Colorado. The Louisiana Purchase substantially increased U.S. territory, and at a rela-

A dinosaur fossil preserved in sedimentary rock that dates from the Upper Jurassic period, roughly 150 million years ago. Many fossils have been found in a rock formation known as the Morrison Formation, which is located in Colorado and Wyoming.

Two miners in their camp on King Solomon Mountain in Colorado, circa 1875. A series of gold discoveries during the 19th century drew thousands of people to the Colorado Territory.

tively low price. The transaction only cost about $15 million, which equalled about four cents per acre. The U.S. gained the remainder of Colorado in the 1840s, after Texas became a state. After the Mexican-American War, the Treaty of Guadalupe Hidalgo granted all rights to the region to the U.S.

When the United States gained possession of this territory, the U.S. government commissioned expeditions to Colorado, with a focus on developing the routes that had been established by the early trappers and fur traders. These "mountain men" had only established the most basic foot paths, but their efforts led to the eventual creation of roads and railway routes that would lead to settlement and economic development.

During 1858 and 1859, many people came to Colorado when gold and silver were discovered near what is now the city of Denver. As the population grew, the U.S. government decided to organize Colorado as a U.S. territory. In February 1861, U.S. President James Buchanan signed a congressional act that created the Territory of Colorado.

In 1863, settlers in the western territories began fighting against Native American tribes, particularly the Cheyenne and Arapaho. Most of the nation's regular soldiers were engaged in the Civil War, so volunteer militias were created to defend settlers. In 1864, territorial governor John Evans appointed a man named John Chivington to command a volunteer cavalry unit.

Chivington believed that it was his religious duty to rid Colorado of Native Americans. In 1864, he ordered his 700 soldiers to attack a village on the Sand Creek in southeastern Colorado. The Natives had camped there because the U.S. government had promised they would be protected. Instead, Chivington's men killed more than 100 unarmed Native Americans, mostly women and children. At first Chivington was considered a hero in the Colorado Territory, but when the truth about the Sand Creek Massacre emerged, he was reviled for his part in the attack. Territorial governor John Evans was forced to resign for trying to cover up the massacre.

The war with the Native Americans ended in 1865, with the Arapaho, Cheyenne, Kiowa, and Comanche tribes forced to give up their lands in Colorado. The Native Americans were sent to live on reservations in the "Indian Territory" (present-day Oklahoma.) Only the Ute tribe remained, with lands in the western part of the state.

The population of Colorado grew as railroads connected Denver and other towns to the rest of the United States. Statehood was proposed for Colorado in the U.S. Congress in 1864, 1866 and 1867, but President Andrew Johnson vetoed the measures each time. During the administration of President Ulysses S. Grant, a new bill was proposed which the president approved. On August 1, 1876, Colorado was admitted as the 38th U.S. state. It became known as the "Centennial State," because statehood occurred just after the United States celebrated its 100th year of independence on July 4, 1876.

Two years later, the discovery of a major silver deposit near Leadville set

Empty buildings remain on what once was the main street of St. Elmo, a mining town founded in 1880 in Chaffee County. The town once had a population of about 2,000, but people left when local mines stopped producing in the 1920s. Today, it is one of Colorado's best preserved ghost towns.

off another mining boom in Colorado. Silver mining remained highly profitable throughout the 1880s, and led to the development of many small towns near the mines.

Part of the reason for silver's value was that Congress had passed laws requiring the U.S. government to purchase a certain amount of silver each year to use for making coins. In 1893, when one of these laws, the Sherman Silver Purchase Act, was repealed, many mines in Colorado could no longer be operated profitably. The mining industry in Colorado soon collapsed, and people left the state in search of new opportunities, leaving behind abandoned, ramshackle "ghost towns."

However, others stayed to establish farms and productive ranches where livestock was raised.

Ranching itself sometimes led to disagreement over who had the right to use public grasslands for grazing. Cattle ranchers had arrived in Colorado first, but in the 1870s and 1880s some people began attempting to raise sheep in the state. The range wars sometimes became violent, with cattlemen occasionally killing both shepherds and their flocks. The tension over grazing rights lasted until the early 1920s.

Despite these conflicts, Colorado continued to grow economically in the early 20th century. Farmers plowed the Great Plains, and even in years when there was average rainfall they could raise huge crops. But in the early 1930s, the national economic depression was made worse for western farmers by a major drought that killed crops and dried up the fertile soil. The farming methods caused soil erosion, leading to an *ecologic* crisis in Colorado and other states known as the Dust Bowl. Strong winds picked up the dried black soil and blew it into terrible storms throughout the Midwest and West. Unable to make a profit, many farmers had to sell their farms and looked for other work.

Colorado was revitalized after the U.S. entered World War II in 1941, and its residents enjoyed greater prosperity after the war ended in 1945. Many people moved into Colorado

View of downtown Denver from one of the Mile High city's many parks.

Did You Know?

Colorado is the only U.S. state to turn down an opportunity to host the Winter Olympics. In 1976, Colorado citizens voted to pass on the opportunity because of the substantial logistical problems involved. They didn't want their lives and communities disrupted.

from states such as Oklahoma and Arkansas.

Meanwhile, the state's geographic diversity provided a substantial new economic stimulus: tourism. The large national parks that Colorado established in the early part of the 20th century gave rise to both a state industry and substantial state revenues. Further, a new wave of new "settlers" that came into the state in the 1960s helped foster an encouragingly swift economic development. Between 1990 and 2000, the state's population grew at a faster rate than all but two U.S. states. From 2000 to 2010, the population grew at an even faster rate, increasing by nearly 17 percent during that decade.

Government

Like other U.S. states, Colorado has a state constitution that mirrors how the federal government is organized: three branches that include the executive, the legislative, and the judicial. Colorado's constitution was drafted in 1876 and ratified the same year. It took effect on August 1, 1876, when Colorado became a state.

The five executive officers of the State of Colorado include the governor, lieutenant governor, secretary of state, state treasurer, and the attorney general. The governor is the head of the executive branch and is elected to a four-year term, as are other executive officers.

Colorado's General Assembly, the legislative branch of the state government includes two houses: the state Senate and the state House of Representatives. Colorado's Senate includes 35 members and its House of Representatives include 65 members. House members are elected for two years while Senate members are elected for two- to four-year terms.

The judicial branch is the legal part of the government. The highest court in Colorado is the state Supreme Court. There are seven justices on Colorado's Supreme Court. Lower courts serve the state's 64 counties.

In the U.S. Congress, the people of Colorado are represented by two senators and six representatives. In presidential elections, Colorado casts eight votes in the Electoral College.

The Economy

During the early 21st century, Colorado was ranked as one of the most prosperous states in the nation. According to an estimate by the Bureau of Economic Analysis, the state's gross domestic product (GDP) was more than $260 billion in 2014, and Colorado was among the fastest-growing states by that measure. Energy extraction was a major GDP growth stimulus.

In the state's early years—before and right after Colorado achieved statehood in 1876—mining was the

The Colorado State Capitol building in Denver houses the governor and the state legislature.

major economic growth stimulus, with mineral extraction being the leading activity. In the late 19th and early 20th centuries, developments in irrigation led to increased agricultural activities—the growth of crops, the raising of cattle—that become another major economic force. Now, the state's leading agricultural products include cattle and sheep, wheat, dairy goods, corn, hay and sugar beets. The state's lead-

The Coors Brewing Company's facility in Golden is the largest beer brewery in the world.

ing export in 2012, according to the U.S. Census, was the meat of bovine animals. As far as mining, the extraction of metals such as gold, silver and molybdenum contribute to the economy. Other leading extractions include petroleum, coal, sand and gravel and uranium.

Today, Colorado has a very diverse economy. In 2013, the Bureau of Economic Analysis reported that other business sectors contributing to the state's GDP included construction, forestry, fishing and hunting, nondurable goods manufacturing, wholesale and retail trade, transportation, warehousing, and finance and insurance. In the middle of the 20th century (circa 1950), manufacturing became a major source of income in Colorado (food processing, computer and electrical equipment, aerospace products, transportation equipment, printing and publishing, and production of fabricated metals, chemicals, and lumber).

Also, the federal government participates in Colorado's economic development. Among the important federal facilities located in Colorado are NORAD (North American Aerospace Defense Command), United States Air Force Academy, Schriever Air Force Base, the National Renewable Energy Laboratory (NREL), the National Institute of Standards and Technology, and the Denver Mint.

In addition, because of Colorado's

natural beauty and diverse geography, tourism is a major business sector. Major tourist attractions include Rocky Mountain National Park, Curecanti National Recreation Area, Mesa Verde National Park, the Great Sand Dunes and Dinosaur National Monuments, Colorado National Monument, and the Black Canyon of the Gunnison National Monument. In 2015, Browns Canyon in Chaffee County was designated a National Monument by the federal government. The state is also home to two of the world's best-known ski-resort towns: Aspen and Vail.

The People

In the 50 United States, Colorado is ranked 22nd in terms of population, with more than 5.2 million residents.

Most Coloradans reside in the area at the eastern edge of the Rocky Mountains. Denver, the state's capital and largest city, is home to about 650,000 people. When the nearby suburbs are included, about 3.2 million people live in the Denver area.

People ski at Snowmass, a winter resort complex in western Colorado near Aspen. Outdoor activities like skiing, as well as the beauty of the state, have attracted many people to Colorado in recent decades, making it one of the fastest-growing states in the early 21st century.

Famous People from Colorado

Lon Chaney Sr. (1883–1930), born in Colorado Springs, was a silent screen actor noted for his appearances in *The Hunchback of Notre Dame* and *The Phantom of the Opera*. He prepared his own makeup and was considered one of the best actors of the silent film era.

Another great star of Hollywood's silent era was Douglas Fairbanks (1883–1939). He was an action-adventure film hero who portrayed such characters as Robin Hood, Zorro, and one of the Three Musketeers.

Douglas Fairbanks

Famed heavyweight boxing champion William Harrison "Jack" Dempsey (1895–1983) was born in Manassa. He was billed as the "Manassa Mauler" because of his aggressive fighting style. One of the most famous athletes of the 1920s, he held the heavyweight title from 1919 to 1926.

Jack Dempsey

A Denver native, John Kerry (b. 1943) is a decorated Vietnam War Veteran and former U.S. Senator from Massachusetts. He was the Democratic Party's presidential candidate in 2004, and served as U.S. Secretary of State during the Obama administration.

Novelist Ken Kesey (1935–2001) was born in La Junta but later moved with his family to Oregon. Eventually, he settled in California, where he wrote several highly regarded novels, including *One Flew Over the Cuckoo's Nest* (1962) and *Sometimes a Great Notion* (1964). During the 1960s he became a counterculture figure as leader of a group called the Merry Pranksters.

Scott Carpenter

M. Scott Carpenter (1925–2013), a lifelong Colorado resident, achieved fame as one of the seven astronauts selected for the Mercury Project in 1959. In May 1962 he became the second American to orbit the Earth. He later set a record by remaining underwater for 30 days as part of the SEALAB project.

According to the U.S. Census Bureau, 88 percent of Coloradans are white, 4.4 percent are black or African American, 3 percent are Asian, and the remainder are members of other ethnic groups. Twenty-one percent of Colorado residents identified themselves as Hispanic or Latino, which is slightly higher than the national average (17.1 percent).

Major Cities

With a population of about 650,000, *Denver* is Colorado's largest city. Situated just east of the Rocky Mountain foothills, Denver is the capital of Colorado.

Because of its geographic position, the "Mile High City" is a *hub* of business activity in the west, and is the home of many large corporations. The

Downtown Colorado Springs is located near the base of one of America's most famous mountains, Pikes Peak, on the edge of the Southern Rocky Mountains.

city sits midway between major Midwestern cities, such as Chicago and St. Louis, and major West Coast cities like Los Angeles and San Diego. Its attractiveness to businesses is enhanced by its convenient access to major highways, railways, and an international airport.

Colorado Springs is Colorado's second largest city, with a population of about 440,000. It is located in the east-central portion of the state and sits about 60 miles (97 km) south of Denver. In recent years, several national magazines have listed Colorado Springs as one of the best cities to live in.

Colorado Springs attracts visitors. The city is close to Pikes Peak, one of the most famous mountains in the United States.

Colorado Springs' thriving economy also benefits from the military and numerous defense and aerospace companies. Major corporations with facilities nearby include Boeing, Lockheed Martin, and Northrop Grumman. Military installations that serve as major employers include Fort Carson, Peterson Air Force Base, Schriever Air Force Base, and the U.S. Air Force Academy.

Aurora, boasting a population of 350,000, is Colorado's third-largest city. A large part of its economy is fed by tourism, as the city possesses more than 6,000 acres of open, natural area. It has more than 100 parks and is home to some of the nation's best municipal and private golf courses.

Colorado's other notable cities include *Fort Collins* (population 155,000), *Lakewood* (population 148,000), *Thornton* (population 128,000), *Arvada* (population 112,000), and *Boulder* (105,000).

Further Reading

Abbott, Carl. *Colorado, Yesterday & Today*. Lakewood, Colo.: Collier Publishing, 2011.

————. *Colorado: A History of the Centennial State*. Boulder, Colo.: University Press of Colorado, 2013.

Collier, Grant. *Colorado Wild: An Intimate Portrait of the Centennial State*. Lakewood, Colo.: Collier Publishing, 2007.

Internet Resources

http://www.colorado.gov/

This Web portal launched by the Colorado state government provides a comprehensive portrait of the state.

http://www.colorado.com/

An authoritative glimpse of everything a visitor needs to know about the state.

www.history.com/topics/us-states/colorado

A Web portal that provides easily accessible information about the state's history.

Text-Dependent Questions

1. Why is Colorado's "Four Corners" designation of interest to tourists, and how does it relate to the state's geography?
2. Why is Colorado called "The Centennial State?"
3. What are four geographic features that characterize the state's landscape?

Research Project

Identify the U.S. President who led the way for Colorado to achieve statehood, and write a two-page report describing why this president was so important a figure in U.S. history.

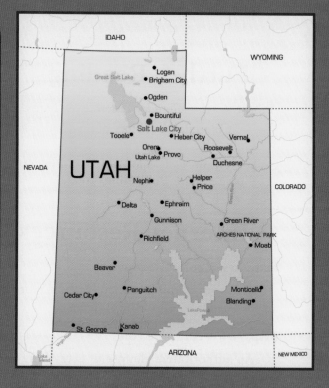

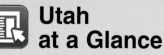 ## Utah
at a Glance

Area: 84,904 sq mi (219,887 sq km)[1].
  13th largest state
  Land: 81,168 sq mi (210,224 sq km)
  Water: 2,736 sq mi (7,086 sq km)
Highest elevation: King's Peak,
  13,518 feet (4,120 m)
Lowest elevation: Beaver Dam Wash,
  2,160 feet (664 m)

Statehood: January 4, 1896
  (45th state)
Capital: Salt Lake City

Population: 2,942,902
  (33rd largest state)[2]

State nickname: the Beehive State
State bird: California seagull
State flower: sego lily

[1] *U.S. Census Bureau*
[2] *U.S. Census Bureau, 2014 estimate*

Utah

The name of the 45th state admitted into the United States union, Utah, derives from the Ute tribe of Native Americans. The tribe's name essentially means "people of the mountains." This is appropriate, as Utah is one of the most mountainous states.

Geography

Utah, which became the 45th state in January 1896, is the 13th-largest of the 50 states in the union. It measures 84,904 square miles (219,887 sq km) that are situated in the Rocky Mountain region of the United States. Utah is bordered by Colorado to the east, Wyoming to the northeast, Idaho to the north, Arizona to the south, and Nevada to the west. Utah's border also touches a corner of neighboring New Mexico in the southeast. It is part of the "Four Corners" region, along with Arizona, Colorado, and New Mexico—the only place in the United States where four states meet.

While its very high mountains are one of the state's most distinctive features, Utah actually has a very diverse terrain, which include desert land and valleys thick with pine tree forests included in three major geographic regions: the Rocky Mountains, the Great Basin (one of the largest *watersheds* in North America) and the Colorado Plateau (which is centered in the "Four Corners" region). Mountain ranges located in the state include the Wasatch Range and the the Uinta Mountains. Other distinctive features of the state's terrain include the Bonneville Salt Flats (a dense *salt pan* located in northwestern Utah) and the Great Salt Lake (located in northern

Utah). The Great Salt Lake is an immense body of water, one of the largest salt water lakes in the western hemisphere, measuring 1,699 square miles.

Touring the state, a visitor will find a high-elevation area in the north characterized by plateaus and basins and a portion of the far-ranging Mojave Desert in the southwest part of the state.

Because of the diverse nature of its terrain, Utah is considered a semi-arid

Words to Understand in This Chapter

archaeology—the scientific study of human activity in the past. Research includes analysis of material that past cultures have left behind.

nomadic—refers to people who move from place to place. Members of nomadic hunter-gatherer tribes roamed to follow the animals that they hunted.

polygamy—a practice in which a man is permitted to have more than one wife at the same time.

precipitation—the condensation of atmospheric water vapor that falls to the ground under gravity. Precipitation includes rain, snow, sleet and hail.

salt pan—a large flat expanse of land that is covered with salt and other minerals.

watershed—an area of land where all of the water under it or that drains off of it goes into the same place.

A mountain lake in the Uinta Mountains. King's Peak, Utah's highest point, can be seen on the left.

The Bonneville Salt Flats in northwestern Utah is encrusted with salt and other minerals left behind when a prehistoric sea evaporated.

Bryce Canyon National Park is known for its hoodoos—odd-shaped pillars of rock left standing from the forces of erosion. The hoodoo at the left is known as "Thor's Hammer."

Utah has a variety of climates, from arid deserts to snow-capped mountains that attract skiers from all over the country. This ski resort is located near Salt Lake City.

state. At the same time, Utah's mountainous regions have a variety of climate conditions. Because of this geographic diversity, annual *precipitation* varies greatly throughout the state. In the dry Great Salt Lake desert region, rainfall can be as little as five inches a years. Conversely, locations in the mountain regions will witness more than 60 inches (152 cm) of precipitation a year, which comes in the form of both rain and snow. The southern valley regions also experience significant snowfall. Temperature ranges can be extreme, with the coldest temperatures in the mountainous regions. Due to high elevations in this area, winters can be harsh. Elsewhere, summers can be hot in the low-elevation areas.

Because of the snowfall in the mountainous regions, coupled with the height of the peaks, Utah is a popular state for skiing, an activity that bolsters that state's economy through tourism. But ski resorts aren't the state's only tourist attraction. Utah is home to six national forests (Ashley, Dixie, Fishlake, Manti-Lasal, Uinta, and Wasatch-Cache), as well as five national parks (Arches Canyonlands, Zion, Bryce, and Capitol Reef). The state also has seven national monuments: Cedar Breaks, Dinosaur, Grand Staircase-Escalante, Hovenweep, Natural Bridges, Rainbow Bridge, and Timpanogos Cave.

Utah's major rivers include the Colorado River and Green River. Besides the Great Salt Lake, the state's largest lakes are Lake Powell and Utah Lake.

History

Archaeologic research indicates that the first people who inhabited the region that became the state of Utah were *nomadic* hunters and gatherers. Archaeologists called these nomads the Paleo-Indians. These people lived in the region as far back as 11,000 years ago. Because it was so long ago, these people hunted now-extinct mammals such as the wooly mammoth (Mammuthus primigenius).

Later, another tribe of Native Americans, called the Navajo, settled in the region. They shared the land with other tribes including the

Goshute, the Paiute, the Shoshone, and the Ute. Like their predecessors, they were also hunters and gatherers. But they became farmers, too, with early agricultural activities forming a major part of their lifestyle. Crops raised included beans, corn and squash. Typically, their living quarters were built within cliffs and in canyons.

These were among the people that the first European explorers encountered when they ventured into the territory. Around 1540 a Spanish expedition led by Francisco Vásquez de Coronado passed through this area, which was claimed for Spain.

In 1776, another Spanish expedition traveled into the northern portion of Utah. This expedition was headed by two Franciscan friars, Atanasio Domínguez and Silvestre Vélez de Escalante. The purpose of Domínguez-Escalante expedition was to find better travel routes between Spanish missions in what are now Santa Fe, New Mexico, and Monterey, California. When the friars encountered Native Americans, they attempted to convert them to Christianity.

During his travels, Escalante kept a diary in which he described the region's natural beauty.

Spain never established settlements in Utah, as it considered the region too dry. However, after Mexico gained its independence from Spanish rule in 1821, it claimed Utah as well as the rest of the American southwest.

Other explorers who entered the territory in the 19th century included fur trappers, or "mountain men," such as Jim Bridger, Miles Goodyear, Jedediah Smith, and Etienne Provost. In 1824, Bridger became the first European to see what would become known as the Great Salt Lake. Because of the size of this body of water, as well as its high salt content, Bridger initially thought that he had come upon the Pacific Ocean. But, through further exploration, he realized he had found a giant lake. Subsequently, other trappers established trading posts in the region. At first, the lake was called Lake Youta, and it proved to be a convenient stopping point for pioneers from the East.

Utah remained Mexican territory

until after the Mexican-American War, The Treaty of Guadalupe Hidalgo, signed on February 2, 1848, to end the war, gave the United States control over much of the American southwest, including Utah.

The Utah Territory was officially created as part of the Compromise of 1850, federal legislation that was intended to avert a crisis over slavery. The name came from the Ute tribe of Native Americans that inhabited the region. The territorial capital was initially established at Fillmore, a town that had been named for Millard Fillmore, the U.S. president at the time. Residents of the territory soon began requesting statehood.

Many of those residents were members of a religious sect that would have an enormous influence on the Utah Territory: the Church of Jesus Christ of Latter-day Saints, also called the LDS Church or Mormon Church.

The LDS Church was founded by a man named Joseph Smith, who claimed an angel had helped him to translate a religious text called the Book of Mormon. Those who believed Smith was a prophet became known as Mormons. They followed him to Ohio, and later to Illinois, where they were

The Great Salt Lake is the largest saltwater lake in North America, covering an area of about 1,700 square miles (4,400 sq km).

Brigham Young (1801–1877) was an important leader of the LDS Church. He had a huge influence on the development of the Utah Territory between 1847 and 1877.

often persecuted for having beliefs that were different from mainstream Christian denominations.

After Smith was killed in 1844, Brigham Young became the sect's leader. He decided it would be better for the Mormons to leave Illinois. In 1847, the Mormons began traveling west. The journey was long and hard. On July 24, 1847, the Mormons reached Salt Lake Valley, where they decided to establish a settlement.

The Mormons struggled to survive in the harsh environment. They created irrigation systems, laid out farms, and built houses, churches, and schools. It is believed that about 70,000 Mormons traveled to Utah in the late 1840s and early 1850s.

Unlike settlers in other states, the Mormons in Utah did not initially have problems with Native American tribes. The lands where they settled did not already have permanent tribal settlements, although several tribes passed through the territory hunting for buffalo and other game. Instead, the Mormons had more difficulty with the federal government, particularly over the practice of *polygamy*, which was permitted by the Mormon religion. Many Americans considered this immoral, and in 1857 President James Buchanan sent U.S. troops to remove Brigham Young as territorial governor. The Utah militia prepared to fight the American troops, but ultimately the matter was settled peacefully when Young stepped down in 1858.

In 1865, the Mormons became involved in fighting with Native American tribes, including the Ute, Paiute, Apache, and Navajo. Over the next two years, more than 100 battles were fought throughout the territory. The fighting continued until 1872, when federal soldiers were once again sent to Utah. Ultimately, the Native

On May 10, 1869, the Union and Central Pacific Railroads joined their rails at Promontory Summit in the Utah Territory. This created the first Transcontinental Railroad, which was vital for the settlement and development of the western states in the late 19th century.

Americans were forced from their land and sent to live in reservations, with the Utes going to Uintah Reservation.

Distrust of the Mormon religion prevented Utah from becoming a state for decades. It was not until after the sect officially ended its support for polygamy in 1890 that the process moved forward. On January 4, 1896, Utah became the 45th state. At that time, nearly 250,000 people lived in Utah. Many were Mormons, but some were immigrants who had been attracted to the state by its mines and other industries.

By the early part of the 20th century, Utah boasted a population as diverse as its topography. Along with Mormons, the inhabitants included people of Greek, Italian, Chinese, Japanese, Slavic and Mexican backgrounds. With regard to women's rights, Utah was more progressive than most of the country. Women were allowed to vote in Utah more than 20 years before they gained that right in every state with passage of the Nineteenth Amendment in 1920.

Utah thrived in the 20th century, in part due to the establishment of national parks and the creation of ski areas. Utah's distinctive dry, powdery snow is especially attractive to the sport's enthusiasts. Tourism was fur-

In 2002, Utah hosted the Winter Olympic games, in which more than 2,400 athletes from 78 nations participated.

ther fostered by the development of a western interstate highway system, which provided easier access to the ski areas as well as the other scenic attractions found in Utah's national parks and its many recreation areas.

Former Utah governor Jon Huntsman is a nationally known politician. He left the governor's mansion in 2009 to serve as U.S. Ambassador to China, and was a presidential candidate in the Republican Party's primary in 2012.

Businesses in the defense, mining and refining industries provided an economic surge after the end of World War II in 1945. Today, industries such as tourism and manufacturing remain strong. Since the 1990s, companies like Novell and WordPerfect have helped make the Utah Valley near Provo a center for technology and software development.

Government

Utah's state constitution was enacted in 1895, nearly a year before the territory achieved statehood. It created a governmental structure for Utah that includes three branches: executive, legislative, and judicial.

An elected governor is head of the state's executive branch. The governor is elected to a four-year term. Other statewide elected offices in the executive branch include a lieutenant governor, attorney general, state treasurer, and state auditor.

The legislative branch is responsible for making laws, and includes the Utah Senate and the Utah House of Representatives. There are 29 state senators, who serve four-year terms. The state's 75 representatives serve two-year terms.

The Supreme Court of Utah's judicial branch includes five justices. These include the chief justice, associate chief justice and three associate justices. Each is appointed by the governor. The judicial branch further divides into district courts that serve the 29 Utah counties.

At the federal level, Utah is represented by four congressmen and two senators. In presidential elections, the candidate that wins the popular ballot in Utah receives six electoral votes.

As in many western or southwestern states, the federal government owns much of the land in Utah. The agencies that oversee federal lands—which cover roughly 70 percent of Utah's total area—include the Bureau of Land Management, the National Forest Service, and the National Park Service. The Utah State Trustland manages public lands owned by the state.

The Economy

In 2014, *Forbes* magazine ranked

(Top) A statue of Massasoit, a Native American who helped the Pilgrims when they arrived in America in 1620, stands outside Utah's Capitol building in Salt Lake City. (Bottom) a crowd gathers at the Capitol to protest air pollution in Utah in January 2015.

Utah first on its list of "Best States for Business." As such, the state has been able to attract corporations, particularly in the high-tech sector, even during the economic recession that occurred in 2008 and 2009. The major sectors that contribute to Utah's economy include agriculture, information technology, medical, mining, tourism, and government services. According to the Bureau of Economic Analysis, the total value of all goods and services produced in Utah is about $131 billion each year.

Coal and petroleum production are major contributors to the state's economy. New technology has made it feasible to extract oil from rocky deposits in eastern Utah. The state also has five refineries, which process crude oil

An oil rig extracts petroleum from beneath the desert in Utah. According to the Utah Department of Natural Resources, in 2015 the state had about 11,200 productive oil wells.

from Utah, Colorado, Wyoming, and Canada. The state is among the top 15 U.S. producers of oil (11th), coal (14th) and natural gas (10th).

A potential future contributor to Utah's economy is renewable energy. Businesses in the state have begun to harness wind and solar power.

Because of the state's great beauty, tourism is another major Utah industry, with visitors coming into the state year-round to engage in recreational activities such as skiing, biking, hiking and camping. In the United States, Utah has the third most national parks, behind only Alaska and California. The state's popular ski resorts are mostly located in Utah's northern section, near Salt Lake City, Park City, Provo, and Ogden.

The People

Factoring in Utah's size (84,900 square miles) in relation to its population (2,900,872, according to a U.S. Census Bureau 2013 estimate), the state is the 33rd-most populous state and the 10th-least populated state in the United States. Most of its people live near the Wasatch Front, the metropolitan region situated in the north-central portion of Utah (which includes state capital Salt Lake City). That means that much of the ground in the rest of the state is virtually uninhabited.

According to another 2013 U.S. Census Bureau estimate, Utah is the second fastest-growing state in the United States. This reason is clear: people are attracted to the prospect of living in Utah. A 2012 Gallup national survey revealed Utah overall to be the "best state to live in" based on 13 "forward looking" metrics related to economy, health and lifestyle.

In its 2010 official census, the U.S. Census Bureau report that 80.4 percent of the state's population was non-Hispanic White, 0.9 percent non-Hispanic Black or African American, 1 percent non-Hispanic American Indian and Alaska Native, 2 percent non-Hispanic Asian, 0.9 percent non-Hispanic Native Hawaiian and Other Pacific Islander, 0.1 percent from some other race (non-Hispanic) and 1.8 percent of two or more races (non-

Famous People from Utah

Utah has many well-known natives, both notable and notorious. Outlaw Robert Leroy Parker (1866–1908), better known as "Butch Cassidy," was born in Beaver. He robbed trains and banks and was a member of the infamous Wild Bunch gang, along with his accomplice Harry "Sundance Kid" Longabaugh.

Also born in Beaver was inventor Philo Taylor Farnsworth (1906–1971), a pioneer in the development of television. He founded the Farnsworth Television and Radio Corporation in 1938.

Philo Farnsworth

Florence Ellinwood Allen (1884–1966), born in Salt Lake City, became the first female judge on a state's highest court in 1922, when she was elected to the Ohio Supreme Court. She later was one of the first women appointed to serve on a federal court.

The Osmonds are a family of entertainers who were born in Utah; all are members of the LDS church. Donny Osmond (b. 1957) and his sister Marie (b. 1959), were the most successful, and today perform their hits in Las Vegas. The other entertainers in the family include Alan (b. 1949), Wayne (b. 1951), Merrill (b. 1953), Jay (b. 1955), and Jimmy (b. 1963).

Entrepreneur John Willard Marriott (1900–1985) was born in Marriott Settlement, near Ogden. He founded the Marriott Corporation, which today owns hotels, restaurants, cruise ships and has annual revenue of around $12 billion.

Educator, author and businessman Stephen R. Covey (1932–2012) was born in Salt Lake City. He is known for his best-selling 1989 book *The Seven Habits of Highly Effective People*.

The Osmonds receive a star on the Hollywood Walk of Fame, 2003.

Hispanic). Also, 13.0 percent of Utah's population was of Hispanic, Latino, or Spanish origin (of any race).

Approximately 62 percent of Utah residents are members of the Church of Jesus Christ of Latter-Day Saints (also called the LDS Church, or the Mormon Church) greatly influences Utah culture and daily life. The world headquarters of the LDS Church is located in Salt Lake City.

Major Cities

Utah's most populous city is its state capital, *Salt Lake City*. The U.S. Census Bureau estimates that about 192,000 people live in the capital. It is located in Utah's Salt Lake Valley. To its northwest is the Great Salt Lake. To its east and south are the Wasatch and Oquirrh mountain ranges. It is a center for government and businesses, as well as home of the world headquarters for the LDS Church.

Utah's second largest city, in terms of population, is *West Valley City*, where about 135,000 people live. The city emerged when several smaller communities were incorporated, and

The Salt Lake Temple is the largest temple of the LDS Church. It took 40 years to construct and was dedicated in 1893.

experienced rapid growth during the late 20th century. Since 2001, additional growth has been stimulated by urban development, including plans to develop a downtown section.

Provo, to the south of Salt Lake City, is Utah's third-largest city with a

Fall colors on Mount Timpanogos, near Provo. The mountain rises 11,752 feet (3,582 m) above sea level.

population of about 117,000. Provo is the home of Brigham Young University (BYU), a private school established in 1875 by the LDS Church. BYU enrolls more than 32,000 students. Provo is also home to the largest missionary training center of the Mormon faith.

West Jordan gained its name due to the city's location on the Jordan River. This suburb of Salt Lake City has a population of about 110,000.

Other major cities in Utah include **Orem** (population 92,000), **Sandy** (population 90,000), **Ogden** (population 85,000), **Saint George** (population 77,000), and **Layton** (population 71,000).

Further Reading

Bancroft, Hubert Howe. *History of Utah.* New York: CreateSpace, 2014.

Till, Tom, and Ted Wilson. *Utah Then & Now.* Englewood, Colo.: Westcliffe Publishers, 2000.

Trueit, Trudi Strain. *Utah.* New York: Scholastic, 2007.

Internet Resources

http://www.utah.gov/government/

> This Web portal launched by the Utah state government provides information about the composition of the state government.

http://historytogo.utah.gov/timeline/index.html

> Launched by the Utah State Historical Society, this Web resource provides comprehensive information about the state including history, facts, government and residents, as well as an historic timeline and a list of the Society's publications.

http://www.city-data.com/states/Utah-Location-size-and-extent.html

> This Internet resource provides facts about Utah and its cities.

http://www.netstate.com/states/geography/ut_geography.htm

> This site provides detailed information about Utah's geography.

www.history.com/topics/us-states/utah

> From the History.com website, this page provides facts about Utah, as well as historic photographs of the state.

 Text-Dependent Questions

1. Why is Utah's state capital, Salt Lake City, called the "Crossroads of the West"?
2. What are the main industries that contribute the most to Utah's economy?

Research Project

Do some research about one of the following important figures in Utah's history: Jedediah Smith, Brigham Young, John Wesley Powell, Daniel Jackling, George Dern, David O. McKay, Reed Smoot, Philo T. Farnsworth, or Jon Huntsman. Write a two-page report providing biographical details and explaining why this person was so influential.

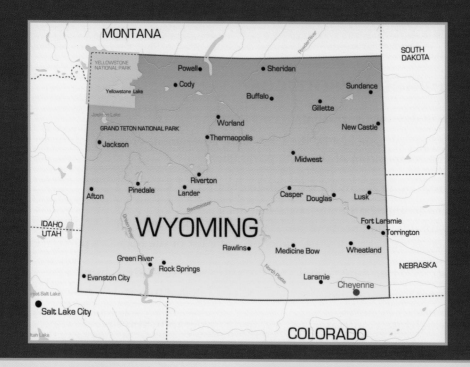

MONTANA

YELLOWSTONE
NATIONAL PARK

Yellowstone Lake

Powell • • Sheridan

• Cody

Buffalo •

Sundance •

Gillette •

SOUTH
DAKOTA

Jackson Lake

GRAND TETON NATIONAL PARK

• Jackson

Worland •

• Thermaopolis

New Castle •

• Midwest

Riverton •

• Afton   Pinedale •   Lander •

Casper •   Douglas •   Lusk •

Fort Laramie •
• Torrington

IDAHO
UTAH

WYOMING

Rawlins •   Medicine Bow •   Wheatland •

NEBRASKA

Evanston City •   Rock Springs •

Green River •

Laramie •
Cheyenne •

Great Salt Lake

Salt Lake City •

Utah Lake

COLORADO

Wyoming at a Glance

Area: 97,814 sq mi (253,348 sq km)[1].
Tenth largest state
Land: 97,105 sq mi (251,500 sq km)
Water: 714 sq mi (1,849 sq km)
Highest elevation: Gannett Peak,
13,809 feet (4,209 m)
Lowest elevation: Belle Fourche River
valley, 3,125 feet (953 m)

Statehood: July 10, 1890 (44th state)
Capital: Cheyenne

Population: 584,153 (smallest state)[2]

State nickname: the Equality State
State bird: western meadowlark
State flower: Indian paintbrush

[1] U.S. Census Bureau
[2] U.S. Census Bureau, 2014 estimate

Wyoming

The name "Wyoming" comes, oddly enough, from the Algonquin language used Native American tribes that lived in the eastern United States. In that language, the word meant "large prairie place"—a decription that is certainly true of Wyoming, but one that also reveals just part of the state's geographic character. True a large part of the state, the eastern portion, is considered *prairie*, but toward the west the state's topography is characterized by mountain ranges that include some of the United States's highest mountain peaks.

Wyoming is nicknamed the "Equality State," because even before it became a U.S. state this territory offered unprecedented opportunities for women, including the right to vote and the chance to fill government positions.

Geography

Wyoming offers a wondrous geographic spectacle with the diversity of its topography. The state is basically an enormous plateau, with mountain ranges rising up from the central and western portion of its

terrain. The land to the east, however, provides a sharp contrast, as it is part of the Great Plains.

The diverse geography of the tenth-largest U.S. state spreads across 97,814 square miles (253,348 sq km) that form a rectangular shape. Wyoming is bordered by Montana to the north, South Dakota and Nebraska to the east, Colorado to the south, Utah to the southwest, and Idaho to the west.

The Rocky Mountains cut through the western portion of Wyoming. Mountain ranges in the state include the Absaroka, Gros Ventre, Owl Creek, Wind River, and Teton mountains in the northwest; the Big Horn Mountains in the north-central part of the state; the Black Hills in the northeast; and the Laramie, Snowy, and Sierra Madre ranges in the south.

Within the Wind River Range are 40 of the state's highest mountain peaks, including Gannett Peak, the highest point in the state at 13,809 feet (4,209 m). The Teton Range includes Grand Teton, the state's second highest peak at 13,770 feet (4,199 m). Grand Teton is popular among mountain climbers.

The Continental Divide—also

 Words to Understand in This Chapter

emigrant—a person who leaves their native country or region to live in another place.

prairie—a large flat area of land covered with grasses and having few trees.

progressive—an approach that embraces social reform or liberal ideas.

retention vote—a vote that determines the status of judges in certain U.S. states, including Wyoming. A judge can be removed from his or her position on a state court if a majority of the public votes against allowing that judge to remain in office.

suffrage—the right to vote in political elections.

called the "Great Divide"—runs along the crest of the Rocky Mountain range, through Wyoming from the state's northwest and down to its south-central border. Generally, melting mountain snow feeds the major rivers of Wyoming. Waters of the rivers on the east of the Continental Divide drain into the Missouri River Basin and ultimately reach the Gulf of

The Yellowstone River passes through the second of two waterfalls before entering the Grand Canyon of Yellowstone, in Wyoming. Yellowstone National Park was the world's first national park. Yellowstone covers 3,468 square miles (8,983 sq km), extending beyond Wyoming's borders into Montana and Idaho.

Jackson Lake, one of the largest high-altitude lakes in the United States, is located in Grand Teton National Park in north-western Wyoming. The lake is fed by the Snake River, and is popular for boating, fishing, and camping along its shore.

The Continental Divide, seen here at Temple Peak in the Wind River Mountain Range, separates the watersheds that drain into the Pacific Ocean to the west from those river systems that drain into the Atlantic Ocean or Gulf of Mexico to the east.

Mexico. These rivers include the Bighorn, Platte, Powder, Wind, and Yellowstone. The waters of the Snake and Green rivers, which are both located in the western part of the state, eventually reach the Pacific Ocean.

Wyoming also has major natural and man-made lakes. The natural lakes include the famous Yellowstone and Jackson lakes. The state's man-made lakes were formed by the Alcova, Boysen, Flaming Gorge, Glendo, Keyhole and Seminoe reservoir projects. Wyoming has 32 named islands located on natural lakes as well as on the Green River.

Looking at other parts of the state, Wyoming's center portion includes a long stretch of high plain. In the southeast, tablelands, or plateaus, meet with the Laramie and Medicine Bow mountain ranges. In the north-

The high plains of Wyoming are suitable for raising cattle.

east, the low-elevation land is ideal for raising cattle.

Because of its natural beauty, Wyoming is home to two of the most famous national parks. Grand Teton National Park is located in the Teton mountain range in northwestern Wyoming. Yellowstone National Park, the first national park in the United States, is also located in the north-west.

Because of its elevation and diverse topography, Wyoming has a climate that is relatively cool. The climate is also considered semi-arid, as precipitation varies—in different geographic regions—from five inches (13 cm) to about 45 inches (114 cm) a year. As far as temperature, residents rarely experience a day that exceeds 100°F (38°C). The amount and nature of precipitation depends on the region. For instance, the mountainous areas receive a significant amount of precipitation in the form of snow.

When it comes to weather extremes, the state's thunderstorm activity is at its highest during the late spring and early summer months. The southeastern section of the state is the area that has witnessed any tornado activity. However, tornadoes in Wyoming tend to be shorter in duration and height and less devastating than tornadoes endured by neighboring states to the east and southeast.

History

The earliest inhabitants of the territory that later become the state of Wyoming were nomadic tribes. These people occupied the land as far back as 12,000 years ago, and they were hunters and gatherers in a land where large herds of buffalo grazed upon abundant prairie grass. Later, Native American tribes living on the land included the Arapaho, Arikara, Bannock, Blackfeet, Cheyenne, Crow, Gros Ventre, Kiowa, Nez Perce, Sheep Eater, Sioux, Shoshone, and Ute. Members of these tribes also were hunters and growers, but they were also skilled in arts and crafts.

During the early 1800s, the first white explorers ventured into the region. These explorers came from Europe. Portions of the region were

This painting of Meriwether Lewis and William Clark conferring with their Shoshone guide Sacagawea includes images of several other figures from the expedition, including John Colter (left). After the Lewis and Clark expedition ended, Colter returned to Wyoming, where he lived for several years as a mountain man.

claimed by Spain, France and England.

The United States gained Wyoming through five major territorial incorporations. The first was the Louisiana Purchase of 1803, when the still-new nation acquired part of the land from France. Other U.S. territorial acquisitions included the Treaty of 1819 with Spain, the cession of land by the Republic of Texas (1836), the Treaty of Guadalupe Hidalgo (1848) after the Mexican-American War, and the Oregon Treaty of 1846, an international agreement with Great Britain that established the U.S.-Canadian border and gave the United States the western part of Wyoming, which at the

Originally established as a private fur trading fort in 1834, Fort Laramie evolved into the largest and best known military post on the Northern Plains before its abandonment in 1890. This restored building, known as Old Bedlam, is the oldest military building in Wyoming, dating to 1849. Behind it are the ruins of other buildings at Fort Laramie.

time was part of the Oregon Territory.

Western exploration and migration increased around the time of the Louisiana Purchase. One of the most important figures in this second wave of exploration was trapper John Colter. His appearance signified the start of an era of vibrant fur trading that would lead to the early economic development of the Wyoming territory. Colter had been a member of the famous Lewis and Clark expedition, and in 1807 he returned to the mountains to live for several years. He kept a diary and wrote about the Yellowstone area and described the now-famous geysers and hot springs. At first, his descrip-tions were deemed too fantastic to be believed. But the explorers that fol-lowed reported that Colter's writings were indeed accurate.

Other mountain men who entered the territory included Robert Stuart, who pioneered the Oregon Trail through the Wyoming territory around 1812. In the 1820s and 1830s, fur trappers and mountain men who lived in the region included Jim Bridger, Davey Jackson, Kit Carson, and Jedediah Smith.

The lure of gold in California and Oregon led prospectors through the Wyoming territory in the 1840s. Following these fortune hunters were wagon trains carrying pioneers who wanted to settle on the U.S. frontier. Native American tribes resented the incursion of whites upon their land and their displacement from their homes. To protect American settlers, the U.S. Army established forts at strategic positions along the trails on the western frontier. The first was Fort Laramie, in southeastern Wyoming, which served as a rest spot for prospectors and travel-weary *emigrants* seeking riches farther west.

Fort Laramie also served as a trading post that fostered commerce in the region, and as a station for the Pony Express and for the Overland Trail stagecoaches that carried passengers and mail to Utah and points farther west. Fort Laramie later proved to be a hub for the cattle industry and the homesteader movement, and around it grew small towns, a sign that a wild frontier was being civilized but in only the most basic sense of that word.

Other important forts in Wyoming established either by the military or trappers included Fort Bridger, Fort Casper, Fort Phil Kearny, and Fort Fred Steele. This fort was built in the 1860s to protect laborer crews working on the transcontinental railroad.

Explorers led by geologist Ferdinand V. Hayden break for lunch in their camp near Red Buttes, Wyoming. In 1871, the U.S. government funded the Hayden Geological Survey, which explored northwestern Wyoming, particularly the area that later became Yellowstone National Park. This was one of several expeditions to explore the Wyoming Territory in the 1860s and 1870s.

View of Cheyenne, Wyoming, as it appeared in 1875.

The discovery of rich coal deposits in southwestern Wyoming attracted the attention of the railroad industry. This led to the construction of a Wyoming route by the Union Pacific Railroad. This line encouraged development of towns along its tracks, such as Cheyenne, which would experience significant growth and eventually become the state capital.

As businesses thrived, settlement increased. The region's population grew, compelling the U.S. government to officially create the Wyoming Territory on July 25, 1868. A territorial government was established almost a year later, on May 19, 1869, with Cheyenne chosen as the capital. Also during this period cattle ranching stimulated the territory's economy and spurred further development. The prospect of statehood loomed.

But before that happened a unique legislative act passed in Wyoming. On December 10, 1869, Wyoming's territorial legislature became the only governing entity in the United States to grant women the right to vote. Subsequently, Wyoming women not only voted but held public office.

The same year that the Wyoming territory passed its "women's *suffrage*" legislation, talk of Wyoming becoming a U.S. state began. However, it would take 20 years before any federal legislative action was taken. In December 1889, bills for Wyoming statehood were introduced in the U.S. Congress. After Congress passed the bill, it was signed by President Benjamin Harrison. On July 10, 1890, Wyoming became the 44th state.

Wyoming's new state constitution was *progressive*. The Carey Act of 1894 allowed private companies to build irrigation systems in semi-arid states and even make money from selling water. The act had the effect of making water use much more efficient. This, in turn, stimulated agricultural development, as water power was used to provide electricity for both farmers and businesses.

In the early 20th century, the state's Progressive political movement gained power and formed a state utilities commission, helped pass a worker's compensation law, and helped the University of Wyoming benefit from

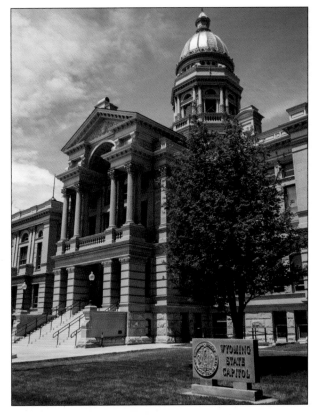

The Wyoming State Capitol was built between 1886 and 1890 in Cheyenne. It houses the state legislature and the governor.

federal grants for agricultural research. During this period, Wyoming also embraced conservation programs.

During the 1920s, Wyoming was the fourth-largest oil-producing state in the nation. In 1924, Americans were outraged to learn that the U.S. Secretary of the Interior, Albert Fall, had accepted bribes in exchange for allowing two oil companies to lease petroleum-rich federal lands known as the Teapot Dome near Casper. This was one of the most notorious government scandals in history.

Since then, however, Wyoming's coal, natural gas, and oil industries have continued to contribute to the state and national economy.

Government

Like many other states, Wyoming's state constitution created a governmental structure that resembles the federal government's in that it includes three branches: the executive, legislative, and judicial.

The governor heads the executive branch. Other executive offices include the secretary of state (which is second in line to the governor as far as succession), auditor, treasurer, and superintendent of public instruction.

The state's legislature includes the Wyoming House of Representatives and Senate. The House includes 60 members, while the Senate has 30 members who represent the state's 23 counties. At the judicial level, five justices comprise the Supreme Court of Wyoming, the state's highest court.

Members of the executive and legislative branches are elected by the public. Court judges are nominated by the state's Judicial Nominating Commission. Their appointment is approved by the governor. But a judge can be removed from his or her position by the public through a *retention vote* process.

On the national level, Wyoming has only one seat in the U.S. House of Representatives. That's because the state is so sparsely populated. Wyoming's one U.S. House seat gives the state just three votes in the Electoral College, which elects the U.S. president and vice president every four years.

Wyoming has an ownership relationship with the federal government wherein much of its land (48 percent, or nearly 31 million acres) is owned by the U.S. government. The percentage ranks Wyoming as fifth among U.S.

Equality for Wyoming Women

On December 10, 1869, the Wyoming Territory passed the first full women's suffrage law in the United States. The legislation could not have passed without the efforts of Territorial Secretary Edward M. Lee and legislator William H. Bright. Both men recognized the important role women had played in establishing frontier settlements. They also claimed that passing the law would help the territory grow. Wyoming was rugged and remote, with a population of more than 6,000 men and only 1,000 women in 1869. If the law passed, they said, it would draw women and families to the Wyoming Territory.

The new Wyoming law did not just give women the right to vote. It also allowed women to hold political office and serve on juries. The year after the law passed, Esther Hobart Morris and Caroline Neil became America's first female justices of the peace. In March 1870, the first jury in the country to include women convened in Laramie. In September 1870, Eliza A. Swain became the first woman in Wyoming to cast a legal ballot in an election.

Esther Morris

When Wyoming Territory's leaders prepared for statehood in 1889, they included a provision for women's suffrage in their constitution. In 1890, Wyoming became the first state to enter the Union with full suffrage for women.

In 1894, Estelle Reel (1862–1959) became the first woman elected to a statewide office. She did such a good job as superintendent of public instruction that many people wanted her to run for governor. Reel declined, but she did go on to become the first woman to hold a high-ranking federal office as the national superintendent of schools for Native Americans.

In 1924, Nellie Tayloe Ross (1876–1977) became the first woman to be elected governor of a U.S. state. She served as Wyoming's 14th governor from January 5, 1925, to January 3, 1927. Ross later became the first woman appointed to serve as director of the U.S. Mint, a position she held from 1933 to 1953.

Nellie Ross

Famous People from Wyoming

Sportscaster Curt Gowdy (1919–2006) was born in Green River. He became famous as the "Voice of the Boston Red Sox" for his on-air work for that major league baseball team. He also worked for the ABC and NBC television networks.

Actress Isabel Jewell (1907–1972) was born in Shoshoni. She was best known for her work in motion pictures during the 1930s and 1940s. Perhaps her most famous role was as Emmy Slattery in *Gone with the Wind* (1939).

Artist Jackson Pollock (1912–1956) was born in Cody. He was an influential painter in the abstract expressionism movement, and he developed a unique style of painting called "drip painting."

Alan K. Simpson (b. 1931) was born in Denver but moved to Cody as a youth. He served in the state legislature from 1965 to 1977, then represented Wyoming in the U.S. Senate from 1979 until 1997. In 2010 he served as co-chairman of the National Commission on Fiscal Responsibility and Reform, which recommended ways to reduce the federal budget deficit and reform the tax code.

Richard B. "Dick" Cheney (b. 1941) embarked on a career in politics after graduating from the University of Wyoming. He represented Wyoming in the House of Representatives from 1979 to 1989; was U.S. Secretary of Defense from 1989 to 1993; and served as Vice President during the administration of George W. Bush from 2001 to 2009.

Dick Cheney

Baseball pitcher Tom Browning was born in Casper during 1960. He won 123 games during his 12-year baseball career (1984–1995), mostly with the Cincinnati Reds. On September 16, 1988, he pitched a perfect game against the Los Angeles Dodgers. It was only the 12th perfect game to that point in baseball history.

Famed actor Harrison Ford (b. 1942) has lived on a ranch near Jackson Hole since the mid-1980s. An experienced pilot, Ford has flown his helicopter on several search-and-rescue missions for the Teton County Sheriff's Office.

states with regard to federal land. Much of the land is managed by the federal government's Bureau of Land Management, the U.S. Forest Service, or the National Park Service.

The Economy

Wyoming's economy is based on agriculture, mining, and tourism. Overall, the state's economy is robust. In 2012, the U.S. Bureau of Economic Analysis reported that Wyoming's gross state product was $38.4 billion.

Mining and the exploitation of natural and mineral resources is the largest sector of the state's economy. Wyoming leads the nation in coal production, accounting for about 40 percent of all coal mined in the United States annually. The eight largest U.S. coal mines can all be found in Wyoming's Powder River Basin.

Wyoming is also among the top 10 natural gas-producing states. Most of Wyoming's natural gas comes from the Green River Basin in the southwest.

The state has only a small percentage of conventional oil reserves, but producers have begun using new technologies to extract oil from large shale deposits in eastern Wyoming. In the meantime, the state has six refineries that process oil from neighboring states, as well as Canada, into gasoline, kerosene, and other products.

Considered a rural state, Wyoming boasts agricultural activity that includes both farming and cattle ranching. The raising of beef cattle and sheep helps supply the nation's food and clothing needs. The state's major crops include alfalfa, barley, beans, beets, corn, oats, and wheat.

Tourism is stimulated by Wyoming's natural beauty. Recent estimates indicate that tourism and travel account for as much as $1 billion added to state revenues. As such, Wyoming is a careful steward of its natural resources, developing programs that protect its numerous national parks and monuments. Its most famous tourist attractions include Grand Teton National Park, Yellowstone National Park, and the Devil's Tower and Fossil Butte national monuments. These sites attract visitors from many countries.

The People

Despite its size, Wyoming is the least populous state in the United States. According to the U.S. Census Bureau, Wyoming's population is about 584,000. However, the state's population is growing, with an increase of more than 14 percent in the population between 2000 and 2010.

So who are the people who choose to live in this state? According to the U.S. Census Bureau, the majority of residents (92.7 percent) are white. Native Americans make up about 2.6 percent of the population, and blacks are around 1.7 percent. The U.S. Census Bureau also found that about 9.5 percent of Wyoming residents are of Hispanic origin.

Wyoming residents are well educated—92.4 percent of adults are high school graduates, compared to the national average of 86 percent. Overall, the state is prosperous. The median household income in Wyoming is about $57,400, which is above the national average of roughly $53,000. Just 11.5 percent of Wyoming residents have incomes below the federal poverty level, compared to the national average of 15.4 percent.

Major Cities

Wyoming's largest city is *Cheyenne*, the state capital. According to the U.S. Census Bureau, Cheyenne's population is about 62,500. The city is located in southeastern Wyoming.

The state government and the military are the largest contributors to Cheyenne's economy. Many of the city's residents are employed at the F.E. Warren Air Force or by the Wyoming National Guard. Many other residents are employed by the railroad companies, including the Burlington Northern Santa Fe and the Union Pacific.

Casper is the second-largest city in Wyoming, with a population of about 60,000. Casper is located in east-central Wyoming near the North Platte River. It is close to Casper Mountain, at the northern point of the Laramie Mountain Range. In 2010, *Forbes* magazine listed Casper eighth on its list of

Devil's Tower in northeastern Wyoming, above the Belle Fourche River, rises 1,267 feet (386 m) above the surrounding terrain. This landmark was considered sacred by Native American tribes.

"the best small cities to raise a family."

Laramie is Wyoming's third largest city, with a population of about 32,000. It is located on the Laramie River, in the southeastern region of the state. The city developed around Fort Laramie in the 19th century. Because of its scenic beauty, tourism is a significant contributor to the city's economy.

Wyoming's other major cities include *Gillette, Rock Springs, Sheridan, Green River, Evanston*, and *Riverton*. The city of *Jackson* (population about 9,500) attracts many tourists, as it is located close to two of the most famous national parks in the United States, Grand Teton and Yellowstone.

Further Reading

Coutant, C.G. *History of Wyoming*. Charleston, S.C.: Nabu Press, 2010.

Dow, James R., ed. *Wyoming Folklore: Reminiscences, Folktales, Beliefs, Customs, and Folk Speech*. Lincoln: University of Nebraska press, 2010.

Holscher, Patrick T. *On This Day in Wyoming History*. Charleston, S.C.: The History Press, 2014.

Lamb, Russell. *Wyoming*. Portland, Ore.: Graphic Arts Books, 2008.

Internet Resources

www.wyo.gov

This website established by the State of Wyoming provides interesting facts, history, and general information about the state.

http://www.city-data.com/states/Wyoming.html

From a site that provides information about all U.S. states and cities, this Internet resource provides a variety of useful facts about Wyoming.

http://legisweb.state.wy.us/LSOWEB/Default.aspx

This site provides detailed information about the government of Wyoming.

 # Text-Dependent Questions

1. Why is Wyoming called the "Equality State?"
2. What are the major industries of Wyoming?

Research Project

Using library and internet resources, find out more about the Louisiana Purchase. Why was this deal made? What impact did the Louisiana Purchase have on the growth of the United States? What impact did it have on the development of Wyoming? Present your findings to the class.

Index

Numbers in **bold italics** refer to captions.

Series Glossary of Key Terms

bicameral—having two legislative chambers (for example, a senate and a house of representatives).

cede—to yield or give up land, usually through a treaty or other formal agreement.

census—an official population count.

constitution—a written document that embodies the rules of a government.

delegation—a group of persons chosen to represent others.

elevation—height above sea level.

legislature—a lawmaking body.

precipitation—rain and snow.

term limit—a legal restriction on how many consecutive terms an office holder may serve.